Fort Loudoun

Winchester's Defense in the French and Indian War

Allan Powell

John Campbell
Fourth Earl of Loudoun

First Printing 1500 Copies

McClain Printing Company
Parsons, West Virginia

November, 1990

International Standard Book Number 0-9619995-3-5
Library of Congress Catalog Card Number 90-91998
Printed in the United States of America
Copyright © 1990 by Allan Powell
Hagerstown, Maryland
All Rights Reserved

Table of Contents

Foreword v
I   Virginia Faces French Expansion 1
II   Braddock Comes to Winchester 12
III Building Fort Loudoun 25
IV Life at Fort Loudoun 36
V   The Indian: Friend and Foe 42
VI Epilogue—A Note About Washington and
      "The Winchester Connection" 53
Appendix 58
Bibliography 62
Word Index 64

Foreword

One of the great losses to our historical and cultural heritage is the decay and disappearance of the many wooden forts, stockades and blockhouses which at one time dotted the landscape of our colonies. In many cases it is difficult to find the exact location of these frontier outposts.

Fort Loudoun, in Virginia, has an especially interesting history because it was designed and constructed by George Washington. This small work is part of my continuing effort to rekindle interest in the French and Indian War by making available an accurate, readable and well-illustrated account of this historic landmark.

Allan Powell
Hagerstown, Maryland
November 1990

I

Virginia Faces French Expansion

The story of Fort Loudoun is an important segment of the larger tale of the defense of the colony of Virginia. This, in turn, is part of an ongoing rivalry for empire between France and England involving no less than six wars which extended over a period of more than one hundred years between 1690 and 1814.

Fort Loudoun was built as part of a colony-wide system of defense consisting of a chain of forts running from the North Carolina border to Fort Cumberland in Maryland. This extensive chain of forts was made necessary because of the devastating raids made by Indians on the outlying settlements. Fear of European expansion and incitement by the French served to encourage the Indians on their destructive forays.

Fort Loudoun is a small, but locally important part of the fourth Anglo-French war—known as the French and Indian War in America and the Seven Years' War in Europe. Formally declared in 1756, this war of international proportions dragged on until 1763, with France accepting a humiliating defeat. Some have even advanced the proposition that this was "really" World War I because of the scope of the conflict. Some outline of this rivalry must be noted before the story of the fort may be told.

Both France and England laid claim to a vast region known as the Ohio Valley—just west of the Appalachian chain. The tension was aggravated because boundaries between various states and territories were far from clear. The clash involved not only France and England but Virginia and Pennsylvania—not to mention the Indians. Needless to say, all kept a jealous eye on the movements of each other.

The actions which provoked the French and Indian War were initiated almost simultaneously. The French had plans to move southward from the Great Lakes to

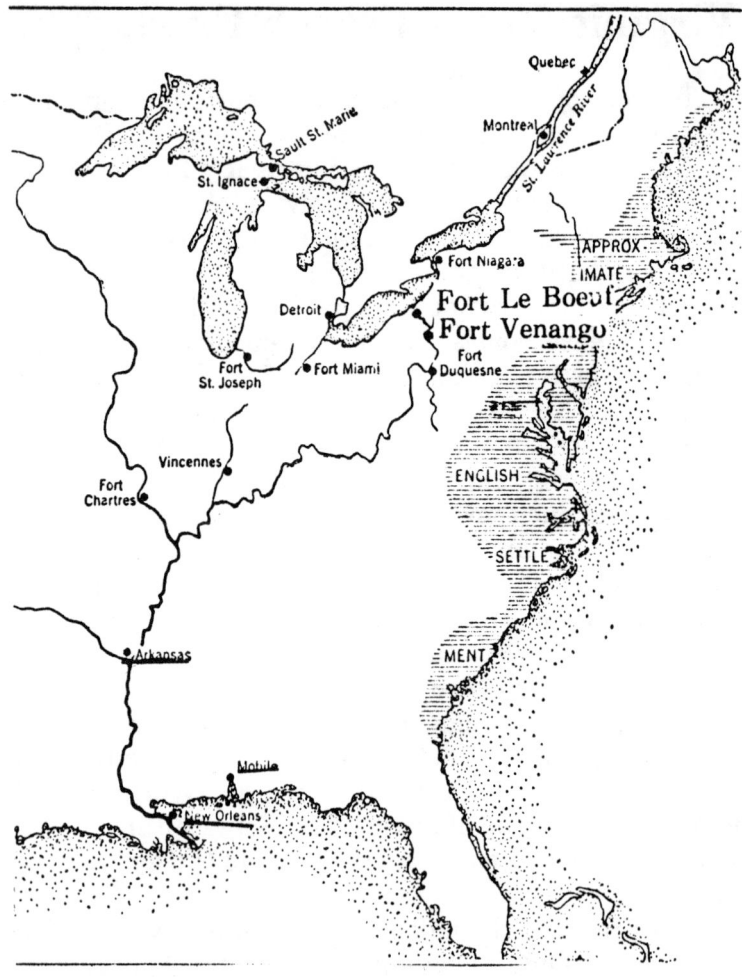

English Settlement and French Encirclement.

occupy the strategic site known as "The Forks" (now Pittsburgh), while land speculators in Virginia intended the settlement of the same region. A clash was inevitable.

As long as the French remained confined to the outer perimeter marked by the St. Lawrence River, the Great Lakes, and the Mississippi River, war might be averted. But both major powers were keenly aware of the importance of controlling the site of the confluence of the Monongahela and Allegheny rivers to exercise domination of the region. Just as the French were unwilling to be confined, the English were also unwilling to be restrained to the area east of the Appalachian chain.

In an effort to reinforce their claims to the Ohio region—claims resting on the explorations of La Salle and the Jesuit missionaries, Marquette and Joliet—a French expedition headed southward from Canada.

> On 15 June 1749, Captain Celoron de Blainville set out from Montreal with a company of 213 men on a round trip of about 3,000 miles. At intervals he buried lead plates inscribed with the French claim to sovereignty. He made formal addresses en route to those Indians who did not run away from his party, demanding the ouster of English traders and threatening dire retribution for disobedience while discreetly avoiding the subject of French sovereignty.[1]

The seven lead plates left no room for doubt about French claims, giving notice "of the renewal of possession which we have taken of said river Ohio and of all territories on both sides as far as the source of the said rivers."[2] By July of that year, forts Le Boeuf and Venango on the upper Allegheny River were completed. (See map page 2). It would only be a short time before another would appear at "The Forks."

Governor Robert Dinwiddie of Virginia received word of these French encroachments into what was regarded

---

[1]Francis Jennings, *Empire of Fortune*, p. 16.
[2]Donald Kent, *The French Invasion of Western Pennsylvania*, p. 7

as territory properly claimed by Virginia. His consequent alarm was aroused because he was a representative of the British Crown which also viewed these actions as a serious trespass. In addition, he was a stockholder in the Ohio Company and faced financial loss should French advances prove successful.

The formation of the Ohio Company of Virginia began when:

Governor of Virginia.

... Thomas Lee and eleven associates petitioned the governor and Council in 1747 for a grant of 200,000 acres on the Ohio River. They met with obstruction, so they adopted a different tactic. Lee organized the Ohio Company of Virginia, petitioned for a grant of half a million acres directly from the Crown, and offered a share in the Company to London's Quaker merchant John Hanbury in consideration of Hanbury's great influence with officialdom.[3]

The tactic was successful. Hanbury presented the company's petition to the king in council on January 11, 1749.

> The petition was approved. On 16 March, 1749, George II ordered a grant to be issued by Virginia's Governor Gooch. But the grant was to contain certain conditions of a nature to arouse a hornets nest. Its provisions required the Company to plant a settlement of 100 families in the Ohio Valley within seven years, and to build a fort for their protection.[4]

This grant gave offense to the French, and at the same time generated hostility on the part of the Indians who

---

[3]Francis Jennings, op. cit., p. 10-11.
[4]Ibid., p. 13.

had regarded the Appalachians as the extent of western expansion for the seaboard colonies. But the British justified the occupation of the area on a treaty with the Iroquois Indians.

Virginia's interest in what has come to be known as the Old Northwest manifested itself indirectly in June and July 1744 at the famed Lancaster Treaty between the Iroquois League and the provinces of Virginia, Maryland and Pennsylvania. In the deed of cession emerging from that treaty, the Iroquois were made to renounce and disclaim all their right, and to recognize the right and title of "our sovereign the King of Great Britain to all the lands within the said colony [of Virginia] as it is now or hereafter may be peopled and bounded by his said Majesty . . . his heirs and successors."[5]

It is not clear whether there was any knowledge about the assumption on the part of Virginia that her claims went from sea to sea because no questions were raised. Also, there is some doubt about whether the Iroquois had the authority to give away lands occupied by other tribes. It is probable that expansion would have proceeded with or without a legitimate rationale since hindsight shows European expansion to have been a surging, irresistible tide.

It is, therefore, with some justification that one historian of the period has leveled the following charge at the land speculators of Virginia. "What must be contemplated seriously, however, is that the needless greed of these few strong men lit a fire in the wilderness that spread to become a conflagration throughout the world."[6] This opinion is not one from the hindsight of historical perspective alone. There is good reason to believe that observers of the day had reservations about the readiness of the Governor of Virginia to commit troops and resources which served to further the interests of the Ohio Company.

[5]Ibid., p. 10.
[6]Ibid., p. 13.

No less an observer than George Washington took note of the resistance to military involvement to protect investors. According to him, the activity toward securing the Ohio Valley, "was yet thought a Fiction and Scheme to promote the Interest of a private Company (by many Gentlemen that had a share in Government).... These unfavorable Surmises Caus'd great delays in raising the first men and money."[7]

It is reported that at least one member of the House of Burgesses of Virginia even went so far as to assert that the disputed region belonged to the French.[8] The forces of expansion were pushing the contestants toward a military solution to their rival claims.

The move southward at first provoked only a warning to the French that their actions were unacceptable. To warn the French that their presence was unwelcome, Governor Dinwiddie selected a youthful (twenty-one years) volunteer, George Washington, to carry the message. The challenge to cover a journey of about nine hundred miles over almost uncharted terrain during the winter months is a tribute to the character of this daring Virginian.

Leaving Williamsburg on October 31, 1753, Washington passed through Fredericksburg, Alexandria and Winchester on his way to Wills Creek (now Cumberland, Maryland). From there, he and his party made their way to "The Forks" (now Pittsburgh, Pennsylvania) and on to Venango—arriving there on the fourth of December.

In his pouch, Washington carried a message, part of which issued the following ultimatum:

> However, Sir, in obedience to my instructions, it becomes my duty to require your peacable departure; and that you would forbear prosecuting a purpose so interuptive of the harmony and good understanding, which his Majesty is desirous to continue and cultivate with the most Christian King."[9]

---

[7]W. W. Abbot (ed.), *The Papers of George Washington*, vol. I, p. 64. All quotations will have original spelling, punctuation, and symbols.
[8]Douglas Southall Freeman, *George Washington*, vol. I, p. 333.
[9]Ibid., p. 26.

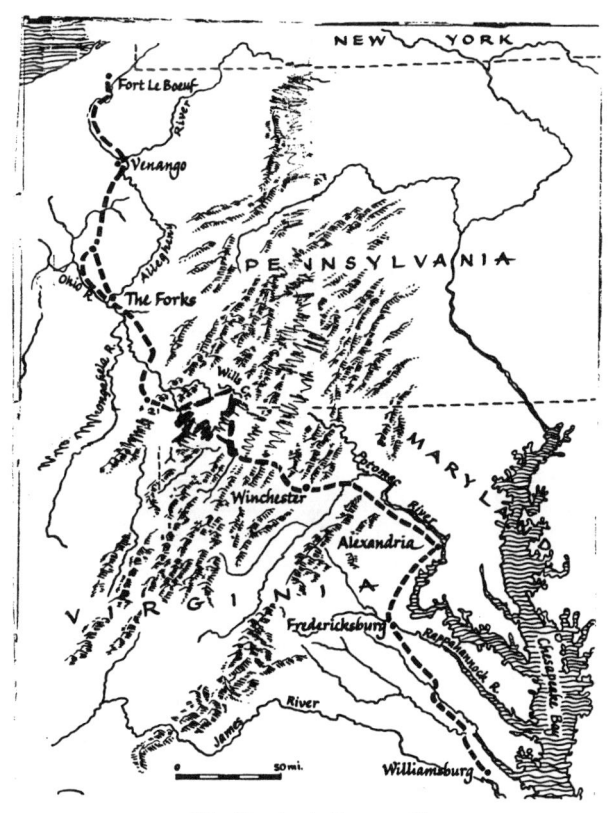

Washington's Journey[10]

Governor Dinwiddie, it appears, did not mince words with his French antagonists.

As it turned out, there was no appropriate official to receive the message at this outpost and Washington was instructed to travel northward to Fort Le Boeuf near the shores of Lake Erie. Before departing as chance would have it, Washington shared dinner one evening with several French officers who, under the influence of drink, betrayed their true intentions regarding the Ohio Valley. Washington relates in his journal that,

[10]Adapted from *Journal of Major George Washington,* pp. vi, viii.

> ... the wine, as they dosed themselves plentifully with it, soon banished the restraint which first appeared in their conversation, and gave a license to their tongues to reveal their sentiments more freely. They told me, that it was their absolute design to take possession of the Ohio, and by G—— they would do it.[11]

Upon arriving at Fort Le Boeuf on December 12, Washington was received by the commander, Legardeur de St. Piere. Appearances of warmth aside, the French officer left no doubt about his intentions to protect French claims. The letter which he gave to Washington to carry back to Governor Dinwiddie advised him that,

> ... as to the sumons you send me to retire, I do not think myself obliged to obey it; whatever may be your instructions, I am here by virtue of the orders of my general; and I entreat you, Sir, not to doubt one moment, but that I am determined to conform myself to them with all the exactments and resolution which can be expected from the best officer.[12]

The French, it would appear, had no inclination to doubt the legitimacy of their claims or their course of action. It would be nine years until they would admit defeat and then only after the failure of arms.

Washington's return to Williamsburg was full of hazards. Luckily he escaped death when his small raft overturned in the frigid Allegheny River. Mercifully he evaded frostbite in the barren wilderness. Again the fates were on his side when a trusted Indian guide shot (and missed) the target—Washington. Overcoming sleet, snow, and falling temperatures, the youthful emissary arrived safely in Williamsburg on the sixteenth of January 1754, and delivered the ominous message entrusted to his care. He also published his now famous *Journal* telling the world the details of his harrowing trip.

Meanwhile, Governor Dinwiddie had lost no time in

---

[11]Ibid., p. 13.
[12]Ibid., p. 27.

preparing to meet the French threat. In January (1754), he dispatched Captain William Trent with some forty men to "The Forks" to construct a fort before the French arrived. Little progress was made before the French, led by Captain Contrecoeur, overtook the fledgling operation. In early April, Ensign Ward's small party was forced to surrender and evacuate in the face of superior numbers. The uncompleted fort was promptly named Fort Duquesne.

Also in April, the Governor was able to get an appropriation of £10,000 to equip the newly promoted Lieutenant Colonel, George Washington, and dispatch him to "The Forks" to give support to the workers at that site. However, when Washington arrived at Wills Creek, he was informed of Ensign Ward's capitulation. He then made the decision to move westward toward Fort Duquesne to clear a road while waiting for more men and supplies to possibly assault the French. His campsite was at the Great Meadows.

While here, Washington received a fateful report that provoked the confrontation which is now regarded as the opening shots of the French and Indian War. A Seneca chief, Half King, informed Washington of an advance party of French soldiers just to the west of their camp. In the early morning hours of May 28, Washington, with his Virginians and some Mingos (Iroquois who had migrated to the Ohio region), attacked the French, killing ten and carrying away twenty-one prisoners. One of those killed was the French leader, Ensign Coulon de Jumonville.

Washington recorded this first military encounter in a journal. He wrote,

> ... fearing it to be a stratagem of the French to attack our camp, and with the rest of my men, set out in a heavy rain and in a night as dark as pitch, along a path scarce broad enough for one man; we were some fifteen or twenty minutes out of the path before we could come to it again; and so dark that we would often strike against one another.[13]

[13]Will H. Lowdermilk, *History of Cumberland*, p. 66.

Washington's victory was fortunate—it would be some time before good luck would come his way again. He returned to the Great Meadows with the flush of victory to ready himself for a French retaliation which was almost certain.

Realizing that he was ill-prepared for a direct confrontation, Washington began to strengthen his position. At the meadows, he constructed a small, circular, wooden stockade which was appropriately named, "Fort Necessity."[14] On July 3, the French appeared in large numbers, led by the brother of the slain Jumonville. After an all-day battle in a steady rain, Washington realized that his situation was desperate. With wet powder, it was impossible to fight; and he had already lost upwards of one hundred men (thirty killed, seventy wounded). The effects of marching and fighting had taken their toll. Their prospects looked gloomy indeed. Washington gave this account of the situation:

> About 9 o'clock on the 3d of July the Enemy advanced with Shouts, and dismal Indian yells to our intrenchments, but was opposed by so warm, spirited and constant a fire, that to force the works in that way was abandoned by them. They then, from every little rising—tree stump—Stone—and bush kept up a constant galding fire upon us; which was returned in the best manner we could till late in the afternoon when there fell the most tremendous rain that can be conceived, filled our trenches with Water, Wet not only the Ammunition in the Cartouch boxes and firelocks, but that which was in a small temporary Stockade in the middle of the Intrenchment called Fort Necessity....[15]

There was no possibility of hiding safely within the small and hastily made stockade because they were not prepared for a siege. As Washington told it, "The Enemy had deprived us of all our creatures; by killing, in the Beginning of the Engagement, our Horses, Cattle, and every living thing they could, even to the very Dogs."[16] In

---

[14]For a well-informed discussion of this fort, see: J. C. Harrington, *New Light on Washington's Fort Necessity*, p. 7.
[15]W. W. Abbot (ed.), op. cit., vol. I, p. 172.
[16]Ibid., p. 160.

a situation where the advantages were all on the other side, it came as a surprise to see a white flag emerge from the woods with its bearer asking for a parley.

Agreement on terms was reached and by one of these, Washington and his battered troops were permitted to leave the site with full honors of war. On July 4, with the band playing, the defeated army started its return march to Wills Creek. This was a most generous gesture indeed, when it is recalled that war was not yet officially declared and that the offer was made by the brother of one who was slain in an ambush hardly more than a month earlier.

The British government was faced with the possibility that they could lose their possessions in North America. Consequently, a plan was developed which provided for two regular British regiments to be sent to these shores under the leadership of Major General Edward Braddock. It is now proper to relate the story of this misadventure before taking a look at the building of Fort Loudoun.

II

Braddock Comes to Winchester

A year and six days would pass after the defeat at Great Meadows before Washington would again engage the French in armed conflict. Again, the French would be victorious. The story of this military disaster has occupied the time and talents of historians since it occurred on July 9, 1755, with only some agreement as to how it could have happened the way it did.

After Washington's surrender on July 3, 1754, the British government determined a strategy which they hoped would turn events in their favor in North America. Two regiments of British regulars were to be transported by ship, and after a tedious overland march, were to oust the French from the fort they had taken at the head of the Ohio River. Two regiments, the Forty-fourth under the command of Colonel Sir Peter Halkett and the Forty-eighth under Colonel Thomas Dunbar were to be under the overall command of Major General Edward Braddock.

Lifting anchor on the fourteenth of January 1755, a large flotilla of transports, ordnance ships and men-of-war set sail from Cork, Ireland, for Hampton Roads, Virginia, arriving there on the twentieth of February. They later moved up to Alexandria where they were to be readied for the long march to Wills Creek and then on to Fort Duquesne. A grand strategy had been drawn up in England even though war had yet to be declared. After the capture of Fort Duquesne—no trouble was expected from that quarter—the army would move westward to Lake Erie, overtaking forts Venango, Le Boeuf and Presqu Isle with little difficulty. The troops would then move on and reduce Niagara—winding up the campaign with the capture of Fort St. Frederick at Crown Point.¹ There seemed to be small doubt that such a vast undertaking would not unfold as smoothly as the pen had committed it to paper.

Major General Edward Braddock.

It was not until April 10 that Sir Peter Halkett was able to leave for Winchester—staying on the Virginia side of the Potomac. The accompanying map shows that Halkett's troops passed within several miles of Winchester on their way to the newly named Fort Cumberland.²

On the following day, Colonel Dunbar's forces marched on the Virginia side of the Potomac to a point opposite Rock Creek. Here they crossed the Potomac into Maryland and from there to Frederick. While there, Braddock dined with Benjamin Franklin who relates the following conversation. "I am to proceed to Niagra; and having taken that, to Frontenac, if the season will allow time; and I suppose it will, for Duquesne can hardly detain me above three or four days; and then I can see nothing that will obstruct my march to Niagra."³ This naivete, combined with arrogance,

---

¹Walter O'Meara, *Guns at the Forks*, p. 110.
²Adapted from Walter S. Hough, *Braddock's Road Through Virginia*, p. 4.
³Lee McCardell, *Ill-Starred General*, p. 174.

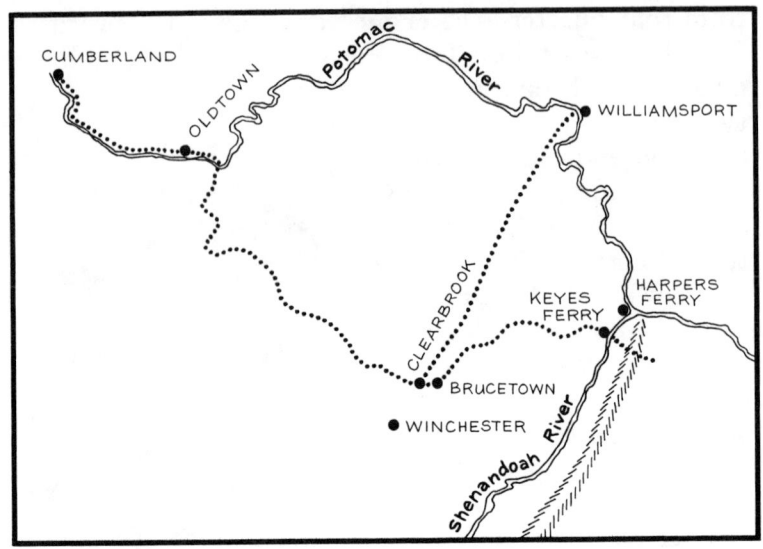

Braddock's Route Through Virginia.

has provided a field day for those who see in these qualities, the main factor in his subsequent defeat.

Since Franklin was well aware of the actual conditions on the frontier and of the terrain over which Braddock would travel, he tried to caution the general about the dangers ahead—especially the Indians. Franklin apprised Braddock that,

> The only danger I apprehend of obstruction to your march is from ambuscades of Indians, who by constant practice are dextrous in laying and executing them; and the slender line near four miles long, which your army must make, may expose it to be attacked by surprise in its flanks, and to be cut like a thread in several pieces. . . .[4]

Franklin then reported that Braddock hastily brushed these observations aside with the ready assurance that,

[4]Ibid., p. 174.

"The savages may, indeed, be a formidable enemy to your raw American militia, but upon the King's regulars and disciplined troops, Sir, it is impossible they should make any impression."[5] As Braddock would sadly learn, "savages" could make quite an impression.

From Frederick, Colonel Dunbar resumed his march on April 29. Ahead lay South Mountain containing several gaps which might be used to reach "Conogogee." Braddock's Orderly Book records this statement, "on the road to Conogogee—17 [miles]." This is followed by "to Conogogee—18 [miles]."[6] But it is far from clear which gap or gaps were used. The record of the stopping points of Braddock's army is clear in Virginia and Pennsylvania—but not in Maryland.

Thomas J. C. Williams, in his *History of Washington County* is quite emphatic about which route Colonel Dunbar used, however. He asserts that,

> The first days march was nearly over the line of the present turnpike road to South Mountain; the army camped at night near the foot of the mountain not far from the present site of the village of Middletown. The next day the army crossed the mountain through Turner's Gap since rendered famous as the scene of the battle of South Mountain. The next morning the march was resumed and the route taken was over the "Devil's Back Bone" at Delemere Mill, and along the present Williamsport and Boonsboro road."[7]

Upon reaching the mouth of the Conococheague, Dunbar's troops crossed into Virginia and on to a point just east of Winchester. From there, they followed the same road used earlier by Sir Peter Halkett. Both regiments were at Fort Cumberland by the nineteenth of May. The accompanying map shows the complete march of the Braddock Campaign.[8]

Another historical figure to meet Braddock at Frederick, Maryland, was none other than George Washington.

---

[5]Ibid., p. 175.
[6]Will H. Lowdermilk, op. cit., appendix, p. xxix.
[7]p. 39.
[8]Adapted from the map on display at Washington's office in Winchester, Virginia.

Braddock's March.

He came into Braddock's service by an unusual route—that of an unpaid volunteer, serving as an aide to the general. Washington had resigned his commission as colonel of the Virginia Regiment in October 1754, because a reorganization plan put foreword by Governor Dinwiddie would have reduced him to a captain. This, of course, was unacceptable to the ambitious Washington.

When word of the upcoming campaign to take Fort Duquesne came to Washington, he apprised Braddock that he would like to serve under his command, but that the issue of rank would prevent his acceptance. In early March 1755, Washington received a letter from Braddock written by his aide, Captain Robert Orme, that he, "has ordered me to acquaint you that he will be very glad of your Company in his Family, by which all inconveniences of that kind will be obviated."[9] The new offer

[9] W. W. Abbot (ed.), op. cit., vol. I, p. 241.

was attractive and Washington accepted with the reservation that it would take some time to clear up some affairs at Mt. Vernon. It was not until early May before Washington was able to make his appearance.

In a letter to William Fairfax dated May 5, Washington wrote that "I overtook the General at Frederick town in Maryland and from thence we proceeded to this place [Winchester] where we shall remain till the arrival of the 2nd Division of the train...."[10] Washington accompanied Braddock and his aides across the Potomac at Swearingen's ferry—now Shepherdstown, West Virginia. After several days, they moved on to Wills Creek.

Winchester, at that time, was a frontier settlement which in 1753 was reported to have had "about sixty houses rather badly built."[11] This visit was to be another of many which spanned a ten-year period in Washington's life between 1748 and 1758.

Both regiments, composed of about one thousand regulars, twelve hundred provincials and about thirty sailors were at Fort Cumberland by the nineteenth of May. The sailors were released from Admiral Keppel's fleet to help move the heavy cannon over the steep mountain slopes. Their skills with block and tackle were useful.

Obviously missing from this aggregate were the Indians. Their scouting abilities would be lost to this venture since only eight were to be on hand at the time of the battle. This loss is attributed to the deteriorated relations which had developed between the Indians and soldiers at Fort Cumberland and because of Braddock's heavy-handed way of dealing with his Indian allies. Indian warriors resented the use of gifts and liquor to seduce their wives and daughters. As the situation worsened, Braddock ordered all Indian women to leave camp. Unfortunately, the braves left camp with them. The final crippling blow came when contingents of Cherokees and

---
[10]Ibid., p. 262.
[11]Ibid., p. 263.

Catawbas promised by Governor Dinwiddie never appeared. It seems that he and the governor of North Carolina were involved in a squabble with the result that he discouraged the Indians from leaving the state.

By May 29, Braddock's army was ready to push westward on its 110-mile march across the mountains to Fort Duquesne. From one fort to the other, a packhorse trail had to be widened into a twelve-foot-wide wagon road. The intense labor required to fell trees and clear boulders made it impossible to move more than three miles a day. Also, moving large guns by horsepower was most troublesome, especially when the horses were weakened by a shortage of good forage. The stoppages were endless and irritating.

By June, it became clear that the pace was too slow and that the army could not reach Fort Duquesne before the expected supplies and reinforcements would appear. Washington reported in a letter to John Augustine Washington (dated 28 June-2 July) that,

> The Genl before they met in Council asked my prive Opinion Concerning the Expn; I urged in the warmest terms I was able to push forward; if we even did it with a small but Chosen Band, with such artillery and light Stores as were absolutely necessary; leavg the heavy Artilly Baggage & Ca with the rear division of the Army to follow by slow and easy Marches....[12]

Thus, it came about that about twelve hundred select officers and men were able to move ahead with greater speed. As luck would have it, Washington was momentarily left behind because he was victim of a bout with the "bloody flux." He had a commitment from Braddock to move him to the front in time for any armed contact. It was in a truly weakened condition that Washington made his appearance on the day of battle. The remaining forces were left behind at what is now known as "Dunbar's Camp," very close to where Washington had had his successful encounter with Jumonville in May 1754.

[12]Ibid., p. 321.

About nine miles east of Fort Duquesne, where Turtle Creek enters the Monongahela, the army would have encountered natural obstructions called the "narrows." Facing the possibility of an ambush here, Braddock made the decision to cross the Monongahela upstream from the mouth of Turtle Creek and then recross the river just below the point of entry.

If there were to be an ambush by the French, it was expected to be at the second fording. But when this did not happen, the expectation existed that there would now be a clear and trouble-free advance to the point of siege. Hopes were now raised to a high level and orders were given to set up for march on the east bank and to march until three in the afternoon. The plan called for rest and a siege to be raised the following day.

The French at the Fort were well aware of Braddock's daily progress. Captain Contrecoeur understood that if Braddock could not be stopped before he set up in a siege position, his large cannon would demolish his fort. Either they must be stopped quickly or they had to evacuate the fort. Contrecoeur seems to have intended to evacuate until his mind was changed by the efforts of a handsome captain by the name of Daniel Beaujeu.

Early on the morning of July 9, Beaujeu, after much pleading, was able to stir up a recalcitrant band of Indians into a hostile frenzy—running to the battle site and directly into a collision with the oncoming British troops. Beaujeu was killed in the initial charge which, nevertheless, ended in success. Another gallant French officer, Captain Dumas, carried on in his place. This was one of those times in history in which one person made a difference.

The tactic which followed was one of an enveloping action which had the effect of completely paralyzing Braddock's forces. It should be noted that while Braddock stubbornly resisted all attempts to adjust requirements of frontier fighting, the French did so with remarkable

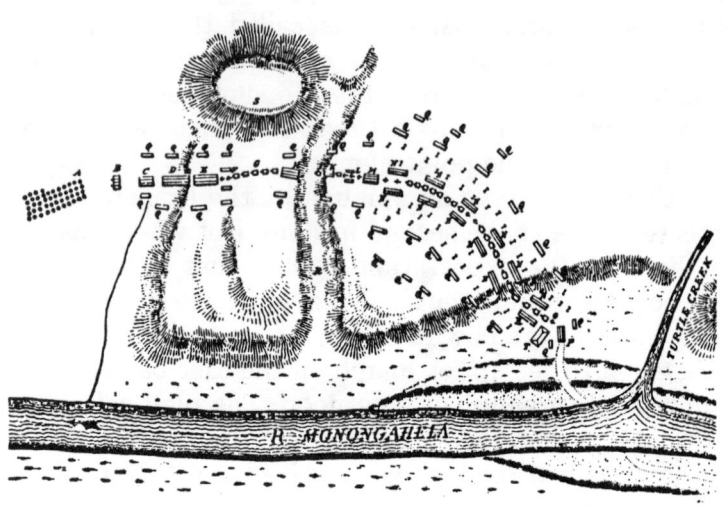

Site of Braddock's Defeat.[13]

success. The above map shows the disposition of troops at intial contact.

It was early afternoon when the collision between the two armies took place. The French and Indians (black dots) worked their way around each side of the concentrated line of British soldiers. For nearly four hours they shot into the huddled mass of uniforms. When the vanguard fell back, they ran in panic into the path of the main body which was being urged forward by the officers. The French had the good fortune to secure the hill which had been neglected by British scouts. From the hill and from behind trees, the French and their Indian allies fired with deadly effect. Surrounded by a screaming enemy they could not see, they behaved as those who are trapped. In order to avoid being an easy target, they sought protection behind other bodies. When they did shoot, they shot into the air or into the backs of the troops in front of them.

[13]From Francis Parkman, *Montcalm and Wolfe*, inside cover.

As the afternoon wore on and no offense could be generated, there was a frenzied dash to recross the Monongahela and on to the safety of Dunbar's camp. Of the more than 1,200 troops who entered the fray on the British side, 63 officers and 914 men were either killed or wounded. As for the French, they entered the conflict with only 36 officers and 72 regulars—supported by 146 Canadians. But they had the able assistance of some 637 Indians—mostly Shawnees, Delawares and Ottawas. Their losses came only to 16 French and 27 Indians either killed or wounded.

Washington came through the battle unharmed, although he reported no less than four bullet holes in his uniform. His courage and leadership were remarkable for one not yet recovered from the baneful effects of dysentery. Braddock was no less courageous having an incredible five horses shot from under him before being mortally wounded. Reports of the battle are a mix of courage and cowardice, brilliance and stupidity, torture and suffering and a considerable amount of embarrassment and finger pointing.

Braddock was carried away on a makeshift stretcher until he came within several miles of Fort Necessity. Here he died—his body being covered in the middle of the road over which horses and carriages passed to remove any telltale signs of a grave. This was to prevent a discovery by the Indians who would have removed his scalp. The body remained at that place until 1824 when it was accidentally uncovered by some workmen. It was then moved to the spot where it is now located.

One of Braddock's officers who was nearby at his death reported that he suffered in silence until just before he died. He then said, "Who would have thought it." And later, "We shall know better how to deal with them another time."[14] These were his last words.

It has been suggested that this disaster could have

---

[14]Ibid., p. 132.

been turned around but for the pitiful behavior of Colonel Dunbar. When stragglers from the battle entered his camp with reports of atrocities, he was overzealous in destroying everything except what could be carried to Fort Cumberland. For one who was so slow in keeping up with the fighting units, he was expeditious in retreat—arriving at Fort Cumberland on July 20.

There is reason to believe that if panic had not set in, Dunbar could have taken the fort. The Indians were more interested in plunder and scalping than in any more fighting. Further, access to captured rum made them in poor condition to return to fighting. It would appear that Braddock should not carry the whole burden for this humilating defeat.

Washington gave his assessment of the battle in a letter to Governor Dinwiddie dated July 18. Among his statements are these: "The Officer's in genl behaved with incomparable bravery," that "the Virginian Companies behaved like men, and died like Soldiers," but that "the Regular Troops exposed all those who were inclined to do their duty to almost certain death, and at length, in despite of every effort to the contrary, broke & run as Sheep before Hounds leavg the Artillery, Ammunition, Provisions Baggage & in short everything a prey to the Enemy...."[15] He then made the serious charge that fully two-thirds of the wounded or killed were shot in the back by their own troops.[16]

There can be little doubt that the whole campaign was a source of embarrassment to Washington. In a letter to a friend he wrote,

> I join heartily with you in believing that when this story comes to be related in future Annals, it will meet with unbelief & indignation; for had I not been witness to the fact on that fatal Day, I shd scarce have given credit to it even now.[17]

[15]W. W. Abbot (ed.), op. cit., vol. I, p. 339.
[16]Ibid., p. 340.
[17]Ibid., p. 350.

It is not difficult to find critics of Braddock who see him as the one most responsible for the failed campaign. Scarouady, a Mohawk guide, had this most unflattering opinion,

> It was the pride and ignorance of that general that came from England. He looked upon us as dogs, and would never hear anything what was said to him. We often tried to tell him of the danger he was in with his soldiers, but he never appeared pleased with us, and that was the reason that a great many of our warriors left him and would not be under his command.[18]

This helps explain the absence of Indians and with it the absence of vital information needed to conduct a successful campaign.

Much has been made of Braddock's character and of his abilities as a leader. It has been maintained that he might well have succeeded if his abilities had been tested in Europe where the old rules of warfare applied. We will never know—history does not always offer second chances. Beside this, the reality was that Braddock was on the American frontier and should have acted accordingly. It is almost certain that Washington suggested adaptation and during the battle asked to alter the style of fighting.

Braddock's secretary and son of the governor of Massachusetts was of the opinion that Braddock was not fit for command. In a letter to Governor Morris of Pennsylvania he asserted that:

> We have a general most judiciously chosen for being disqualified for the service he is employed in almost every respect. ... I am greatly disgusted at seeing an expedition (as it is called) so ill conceived originally in England, and so ill appointed, so improperly conducted since in America.[19]

Others saw Braddock as "a man of weak understanding, positive, and very indolent, Slave to his passions, women & wine, as great an Epicure as could be in his eat-

---
[18]Lee McCardell, op. cit., p. 263.
[19]W. W. Abbot (ed.), op. cit., vol. I, p. 248.

ing, though a brave man."[20] These criticisms are not mere personality differences, they are substantive qualities which affect the quality of leadership.

Returning to Colonel Dunbar, we encounter another disastrous decision that he made. After only a brief stay at Fort Cumberland, he made good on his plan to march to Philadelphia and set up "winter" quarters there—in August. On the second of that month, Dunbar left the frontier to fend for itself. With the army gone and Fort Cumberland populated mostly with sick, wounded and dying, the frontier portion of each colony was open to assault and ravaging by a merciless horde of Indians, goaded on by presents and rum, all supplied by their French beneficiaries. The short-term consequence was much personal suffering. The long-term results meant that it would be another three years before a British flag would fly over Fort Duquesne.

[20]Ibid., p. 348.

III

Building Fort Loudoun

Virginia's frontier was as open to attack as those of the other colonies after the defeat of Braddock at the Monongahela on July 9, 1755. The situation was worsened by the abdication of the backcountry by Colonel Thomas Dunbar in August of the same year.

Until the formation of the Virginia Regiment under the command of Colonel George Washington in September 1755, the "back inhabitants" were protected from the incoming Indians by several companies of rangers. These forces were supplemented in local crises by militia—when they could be raised.[1] Yet it was almost one year before the construction of a substantial fort would be started.

In the meantime, small stockades, fortified houses and blockhouses were the main source of defense on the Virginia frontier. That these were inadequate to the task is an understatement as reports of the boldness of Indian encroachments make clear. Nor were the inhabitants reliable in the defense of their houses and property. Fortunately, the youthful Washington was both able and ambitious enough to return the frontier to safety. But the Indian raids were to continue from the time of Braddock's defeat until the Indians were eventually subdued and pushed westward by Colonel Henry Bouquet after the battle of Bushy Run in 1763.

[1] W. W. Abbot (ed.), *The Papers of George Washington*, vol. II, p. 90.

On August 14, 1755, Governor Robert Dinwiddie appointed Washington, "Colonel of the Virga. Regimt & Commander in Chief of all the Forces now rais'd & to be rais'd for the Defense of this H: Majesty's Colony; & for repellg the unjust & hostile Invasions of the Fr. & their Indn Allies...."[2] The same letter ordered Washington to make Winchester his base of operations because "as Winchester is the highest Place of rendezvous to the Country which is exposed to the Enemy, You are hereby required to make that Your head Quarters."[3]

Even though his rank and pride had been restored, Washington would still face challenges to his command. In an attempt to strengthen his position, he imposed several demands on the Governor as conditions of acceptance. One of these was a "military chest" or general fund to be used for contingencies at his discretion. Another was the power to hire two assistants; one to be an aide-de-camp, the other to be a secretary. Finally, he wanted to appoint his own field officers.[4]

The new commander in chief arrived at Winchester on September 14, and immediately began the enormous task of building a colonial army. Before setting out, Washington issued some "General Instructions For Recruiting" to be followed. One of the more interesting ones required,

> That no Officer shall list any men under Sixteen, or above Fifty years of age: nor are they to list men under five feet four high, unless they are well made, strong, and active then, and in that case, they will be received.
>
> Neither are they to list any men who have old Sores upon their legs, or who are subject to Fits; which will be inspected into by the Surgeons, upon their arrival at Quarters: and such as are found to come under these articles will be discharged....[5]

[2]Ibid., p. 4.
[3]Ibid., p. 5.
[4]See Douglas Southall Freeman, *George Washington*, vol. II, pp. 112-13.
[5]W. W. Abbot (ed.), op. cit., vol. II, p. 13.

Conditions at Winchester were appalling. Adam Stephen, reporting about the status of security from Fort Cumberland, declared that, "The Smouk of Burning Plantations darken the day and hide the neighboring mountains from our Sight."[6] Washington stated that, ". . . I arrived yesterday aft Noon, and found everything in the greatest hurry and confusion by the back Inhabitants flocking in, and those of the Town removing out, which I have prevented as far as it was in my power."[7] He then added that scouts hired to bring in reports of Indian activity estimated that about 150 Indians were then in the area and that about 70 people had been killed while their houses and plantations had been destroyed.[8]

During the winter of 1755-56, Washington faced an important challenge to his authority which eclipsed, in his mind, the daily problems of protecting the frontier. The incident began when the commander at Fort Cumberland, Colonel James Innes, requested leave to take care of some personal matters in North Carolina. The command of the fort was delegated to Lieutenant Colonel Adam Stephen—who was accountable to Washington.

It should be kept in mind, that while Fort Cumberland was located in Maryland, it was a "King's Fort" and under the control of the governor of Virginia who had it built on orders from the king. Nonetheless, a small contingent of Maryland troops were dispatched to the fort by the Governor of Maryland, Horatio Sharpe, and under the command of Captain John Dagworthy. Stephen was unable to take effective command because Captain Dagworthy simply asserted that he was the rightful post commander. This claim rested on the assumption that in his earlier military career he had held a royal commission and that this superceded in authority any colonial commission. The issue went unresolved for

[6]Ibid., p. 12.
[7]Ibid., p. 101.
[8]Ibid., p. 104.

months and fort operations and relationships deteriorated.

Finally, Washington requested leave to approach Major General William Shirley directly, even though this required a trip of more than nine hundred miles on horseback and ship to Boston during the worst part of the winter season. Governor Dinwiddie, who was equally irate on account of this Maryland upstart, gave his permission and with it a note of support to show General Shirley. It read,

> This Fort was built by virtue of His Majesty's instructions to me, and by my orders to Col. James Innes, then in the pay of this Colony, and with a great charge to this Country. Its true it happens to be in Maryland, but I presume His Majesty has a right to build a Fort where he pleases in any of his Colonies; and the guns mounted are sent by His Majesty for the service of Virginia; it cannot be reasonably suggested that His Majesty intended them for the Proprietary of Maryland.[9]

After reading the opinion of the governor and hearing the firsthand report of the situation, General Shirley resolved the issue abruptly—in Washington's favor. In an order dated March 5, 1756, he declared, "It is My Orders that Colonel Washington should take command."[10] This was followed by a letter to Governor Sharpe which left him no options. "I must desire that Cap. Dagworthy may be removed from Fort Cumberland; or acquainted that if he remains there, he must put himself under the command of Colonel Washington."[11]

With the return of spring 1756, new Indian troubles erupted. Reports of small Indian raiding parties increased. Washington seemed overwhelmed and personally saddened by the amount of suffering made known to him. In a most touching appeal for help, he wrote to the Governor from Winchester dated April 1756.

---

[9]W. W. Abbot (ed.), op. cit., vol. II, p. 291.
[10]W. W. Abbot (ed.), Ibid., vol. II, p. 323.
[11]Ibid., p. 324.

> Your Honor may see to what unhappy straits the distressed Inhabitants as well as I, am reduced. I am too little acquainted, Sir, with pathetic language, to attempt a description of the peoples distresses; though I have a generous soul, sensible of wrongs, and swelling for redress—But what can I do? If bleeding, dying! would glut their insatiate revenge—I would be a willing offering to Savage Fury: and die by inches, to save a people! I see their situation, know their danger, and participate their suffering; without having it in my power to give them further relief, than uncertain promises.[12]

This personal appeal was followed by two letters, both written in late April, to the speaker of the House of Burgesses and later to the governor. In each, there is a strong recommendation for a chain of forts on the frontier of Virginia with "a large and strong Fort at this place [Winchester], to serve as a Receptacle for all our Stores & C. and a place of Refuge for the Women and Children in times of danger."[13]

Meanwhile, progress was being made in Williamsburg. In March, an act had been passed by the House of Burgesses to provide for the defense of Winchester. In part it read,

> And whereas it is now judged that a fort should be immediately erected in the town of Winchester, in the county of Frederick, for the protection of the adjacent inhabitants from the barbities daily committed by the French and their Indian allies, Be it enacted by the authority aforesaid, that the governor, or commander in chief of this colony for the time being, is hereby empowered, and desired to order a fort to be built with all possible dispatch in the aforesaid town of Winchester.[14]

Washington would later name the fort in honor of John Campbell, fourth Earl of Loudoun, the incoming commander of all colonial forces in North America who arrived in New York in July 1756.

After legislative approval, barely two months were to

---

[12]W. W. Abbot (ed.), op. cit., vol. III, p. 33.
[13]Ibid., p. 60.
[14]J. E. Norris, *History of the Lower Shenandoah Valley*, p. 112.

pass before Washington would begin construction. On May 18, Washington advised Adam Stephen at Fort Cumberland that,

> I am also detained here to Construct and erect a fort, which the Governor has ordered to be done with expedition—as it will be necessary to have a number of Carpenters, & C. to carry on the work with spirit, and vigour: you are desired to send down all the men of Captain George Mercers Company; those that are there of Captain Bells—all the men that are really skilled in masonry: and if all these do not make up fifty—you are to complete the party to that number out of the best Carpenters in other Companies.[15]

Frontier Forts in Virginia.[16]

[15] W. W. Abbot (ed.), op. cit., vol. III, p. 157.
[16] Adapted from Freeman, op. cit., p. 229.

Then, on May 23, Washington reported to the Governor from Winchester that, "at this place I have begun the Fort according to your Orders, and found, as little of the matter as I know myself, the work could not be conducted if I was away: which was one among many reasons, that detained me here."[17]

It appears that Washington drew two sets of plans for the intended fort at Winchester. Two plans are mentioned in a letter from William Fairfax of Belvoir to Washington dated July 10, 1756. Fairfax makes several suggestions to improve the design.[18] This is supported by the fact that

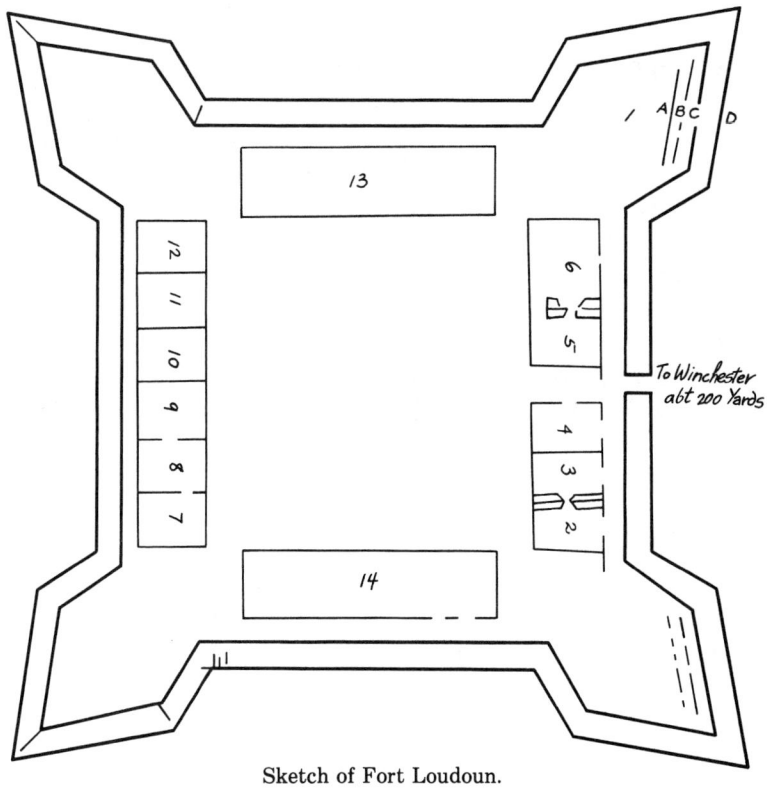

Sketch of Fort Loudoun.

[17] W. W. Abbot (ed.), op. cit., vol. III, p. 173.
[18] Ibid., p. 247.

the Library of Congress also has two different designs of the fort. One of the sketches is reproduced here.

Fort Loudoun was not a large fort in that it only enclosed one-half acre. By comparison, both Fort Cumberland and Fort Frederick enclosed one and one-half acres of ground. The length of each curtain was ninety-six feet with bastion faces and flanks twenty-five feet long.[19] Yet there are repeated claims that the fort was planned to house as high as five hundred troops. This is more than one would expect when it is noted that the two larger forts mentioned were built to accommodate about two hundred troops.

As for armaments, Fort Loudoun had an impressive array of guns for defense; this included six 18-pounders, six 12-pounders, six 6-pounders, four swivels and two howitzers.[20] Water for the fort came from a well said to have been blasted through solid rock to a depth of 103 feet. It can still be seen in the backyard of a home on Loudoun Street in Winchester. The water, unfortunately, is presently unsafe to drink.

It is unclear how the actual walls of the fort were constructed. An early visitor to the fort, the Reverend Andrew Barnaby, claimed that his 1760 description revealed that "The materials of which it is constructed are logs filled with earth; the soldiers attempted to surround it with a dry ditch; but the rock was so extremely hard and impenetrable that they were obliged to desist."[21] This was then interpreted to be, "Parallel rows of upright logs, the rows being about two feet apart, the space being filled with dirt, made up the outer wall. Inside of this barrier another palisade of upright logs was erected, thus making a double defense."[22] If this description is correct, it is

---

[19]T. K. Cartmell, *Shenandoah Valley Pioneers and Their Descendants*, p. 130.

[20]Ibid., p. 130.

[21]Garland R. Quarles, *George Washington and Winchester, Virginia, 1748-1758*, p. 29.

[22]William H. Ansel, Jr., *Frontier Forts Along the Potomac and Its Tributaries*, p. 122.

most unusual in view of the fact that Washington had visited other forts, such as Fort Cumberland, which were constructed of single rows of logs. Fort Cumberland used single logs—eighteen feet in length—sunk into the earth to a depth of six feet.

Kercheval declared that an early settler of Winchester having direct acquaintance with several of Washington's officers assured him that, "Washington marked out the site of the Fort, and superintended the work; that he bought a lot in Winchester, erected a smith's shop on it, and brought from Mount Vernon his own blacksmith to make the necessary iron work for the fort."[23] The site selected for the fort was northernmost of two hills in the town of Winchester. The hill to the south had the distinctive name of "Potato Hill" while the other came to be called "Fort Hill," for obvious reasons.[24] Work on the fort must have progressed slowly because it was still not completed by the spring of 1758. Periodic statements over the two-year span by Washington indicate an impatience to be done with the project. However, the fort was functioning in the rough well before the later date.

One can get a sense of Washington's frustration from a report to the governor a little more than a year after the fort construction got underway.

> We are indefatigably assiduous in forwarding the workmen; All work from daylight to daylight, Sundays not accepted, and but one hour in the day allowed for eating, etc. But it is impossible that so small a number of men as we have had and how have at work, can be imagined sufficient to complete such a vastly heavy piece of work in a much greater time than you mention. Nay, 300 men could hardly finish it by next October.[25]

Almost another year would elapse and Washington now advised John Blair (Fort Loudoun, May 24, 1758),

---

[23]Samuel Kercheval, *A History of the Valley of Virginia*, p. 70.
[24]John W. Wayland, *Twenty-Five Chapters on the Shenandoah Valley*, p. 126.
[25]W. W. Abbot (ed.), vol. IV, pp. 264-65.

"If the works here are to be completed, which from their great importance I should think highly necessary, in that event, an additional number of 60 or 80, good men from the militia, for that particular service would be wanted."[26]

Contemporary reports indicate that Fort Loudoun was never directly attacked even though skirmishes with the Indians occurred frequently in the general vicinity of the fort. On one occasion the fort was said, "to have been reconnoitered by French officers and found impregnable."[27] This must have discouraged the small raiding parties from being foolhardy. But, it should be remembered that to the north in other states, larger forts were not immune from attacks.

It is not clear whether Fort Loudoun was used to house prisoners of war during the American Revolution. There is reason to believe that, because of deterioration, other forms of housing were used. A Hessian officer who was a prisoner of war in Winchester in 1777 wrote that there "can still be seen the remains of the fort where George Washington, then Colonel, Commanded and himself defended."[28] This same historian asserted that, "a formal barracks for prisoners, as stands today in Frederick, never existed in Winchester. Instead, the Americans built a number of temporary huts four miles west of town in the village of Round Hill. These structures quickly disappeared after the war."[29]

In any case, gradual deterioration did take place and by the time of the Civil War, not much remained. In 1864, James E. Taylor, an artist for Frank Leslie's *Illustrated Newspaper* sketched three scenes of interest about Fort Loudoun. One depicts a soldier at the well which was still being used. Another sketch shows a re-

---

[26]W. W. Abbot (ed.), vol. V, pp. 157-58.
[27]Garland R. Quarles, op. cit., p. 29.
[28]Lion G. Miles, "The Winchester Hessian Barracks," p. 25.
[29]Ibid., p. 21.

maining bastian. Finally, there is an overhead sketch of the fort site showing where Loudoun Street was cut through the old structure.[30]

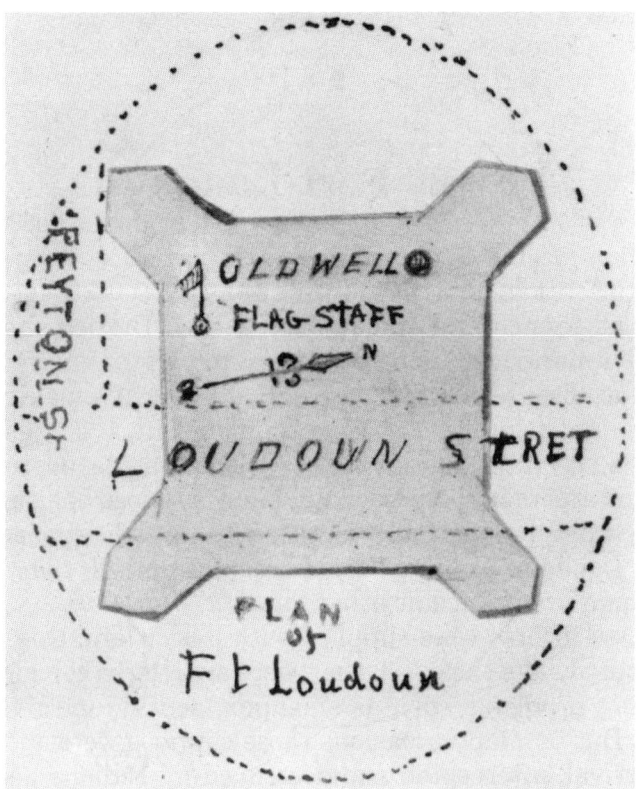

It is now appropriate to try to recapture what life was like for those who lived in and around Fort Loudoun. It served its purpose well during two major periods of Indian incursions; first after the defeat of Braddock and then during the period of turmoil in 1763, since known as Pontiac's Conspiracy. But the passage of time has dealt Fort Loudoun the same fate as most other wooden forts of the French and Indian War era.

[30]*The James E. Taylor Sketchbook,* p. 566. For a similar, but recent sketch, see appendix, p. 4.

IV

Life at Fort Loudoun

There seems to have been little variation from one frontier fort to another in terms of living conditions during the French and Indian War period. Diaries and official reports are replete with accounts of overwork, fatigue, disease, torture, boredom, scarcity of female company, snakebites, excessive punishment, "chiggers," poison ivy, drabness, extremes of temperature, desertion and interpersonal friction. We must suppose that aside from what was actually reported to have happened at Fort Loudoun, it experienced much, if not all, that was common occurrence at other forts.

Even if forts were supplied with basics (and this was seldom always the case), they were subject to certain recurring problems such as smallpox, scurvy and dysentery. But on many occasions these supplies were spoiled on arrival, intercepted and destroyed by Indians before arrival or even destroyed after arrival to keep the enemy from getting them.

Correspondence between fort commanders and public officials frequently mention that they are afflicted with a bout of some disease, large numbers of desertions, a straggler being killed after wandering too far from the protective walls of the fort or a truly pathetic account of a lashing for drunkenness or swearing.

A look at the daily rations given to each soldier will show the source of many problems. But it would be an error to suppose that even this most restricted diet was always available. The following ration list was issued to Henry Bouquet by Lord Loudoun.[1]

The Contractors are Obliged to furnish the following proportions for each Soldier
Bread pr week 7 pound — or same quantity of flower
Beef d/o   7 pound — In lieu thereof 9 pound of pork
Peas d/o   3 pints — or half that quantity of Rice

Of course these rations might be supplemented by berries, nuts and other choices at the various fort sites or with meat supplied by Indians who were friendly. But these could not be counted on with any degree of assurance. The French were more adept at survival in the woods than the British forces. A lack of these skills accounted for much suffering on the frontier.

Some fort commanders encouraged gardens near their fort as a means to ward off scurvy. Eventually, a spruce beer was discovered that was helpful in controlling breakouts of this disease. Spruce beer was brewed by taking tender sprigs of spruce twigs and boiling them in water for three hours. The broth was then mixed with molasses (one quart per six gallon) and then allowed to ferment for twelve days in wooden kegs. This beverage was declared to be effective.

Inadequate diet was more than matched by uncleanliness as a source of sickness. Large numbers of soldiers were plagued with dysentery or "bloody flux" as it was called. Forts were not very clean and cooking utensils fared little better. Washington suffered two long bouts of dysentery (one already mentioned on the Braddock campaign in 1755) and another one during the late summer and fall of 1757. Beginning in July, the misery increased until November. By this time, Washington was so weak he could barely walk. In early November, under doctor's orders, he left Winchester for treatment in Alexandria.[2]

[1]S. K. Stevens, et. al. (eds.), *The Papers of Henry Bouquet,* p. 65.
[2]Freeman, op. cit., vol. II, pp. 274-75.

General Forbes, who directed the campaign against the French to take Fort Duquesne in 1758, suffered from this malady throughout the entire campaign. He was so weak that he could not be moved except occasionally on a makeshift, horse-pulled litter made for him. He died soon after the campaign ended. But if officers were not immune from this scourge, it is even more likely to affect enlisted men, who cooked their own meals. Recruits were drawn from the lower ranks of society—often they are referred to as "riff-raff" or the "dregs" of society. It is certain that sanitation was not one of their priority items.

Another disease which struck with devastating effects was smallpox—leaving many forts with large numbers of deaths. In this regard, Washington was singularly fortunate. He survived the disease which he contracted while traveling with his half-brother Lawrence before he began his military career. He was now immune from this disease and was unaffected as he came into contact with others on the frontier.

With a shortage of doctors at each fort, it was not possible to get proper treatment even at the best of times. During and after a battle, or during a siege, the conditions were intolerable. Also, medical practice was relatively primitive, thus adding to the problem.

Alongside these sources of suffering was another that exacted a heavy toll at forts. Punishment was unbelievably inhumane. Confinement, even under grizzly conditions was generous compared to the liberal use of the whip or the death sentence. In this regard, Washington was a strict disciplinarian, exhibiting the same attitudes as other civil and military leaders of the day. Several examples will serve to illustrate the point. On May 1, 1756, at Winchester, Washington issued the following order.

> Any Soldier, who shall presume to quarrel or fight; shall receive five hundred lashes, without the benefit of a Court Martial. The Offender upon Complaint made shall have strict justice done him.

> Any Soldier found Drunk, shall immediately receive one hundred lashes; without Benefit of a Court-martial.[3]

Only two days later, Washington wrote to Governor Dinwiddie asking him to give his approval for a death sentence. He wrote,

> I inclose your Honor the Sentence of a General Court Martial, which was held here upon a Sergeant for running away with his Party. They have, I think, very justly adjudged him to suffer Death; which sentence I hope you approve of; as there never was a fitter object to make an Example of—being the second time he has been guilty of the same crime....[4]

The governor speedily approved of this sentence and issues a death warrant, "... that he may be a public Example to deter others from such like Offenses."[5] This should not be taken to be an isolated instance. In another letter to the governor, Washington apprised him of another hanging and with the same justification. He wrote,

> I send Your Honor a copy of the proceedings of a General Court martial. Two of those condemned, namely Ignatius Edwards and Wm. Smith, were hanged on Thursday last, just before the companies marches for their respective posts. Your Honor will, I hope excuse my hanging, instead of shooting them: It conveyed much more terror to others; and it was for example sake, we did it....[6]

One is surprised, in the light of such harsh discipline, that the number of desertions and other infractions did not decline. Fear of harsh punishment was believed by all to be the prime deterrent of deviancy—but it is far from clear as to whether this assumption was correct. Braddock's Orderly Book also gives evidence of the acceptance of severe discipline, some which makes the reader cringe. "Any Soldier who shall desert tho' he return again will be hanged without mercy."[7] Or, "Any

---

[3]W. W. Abbot (ed.), op. cit., vol. III, p. 70.
[4]Ibid., p. 84.
[5]Ibid., p. 103.
[6]W. W. Abbot (ed.), op. cit., vol. IV, p. 360.
[7]Will H. Lowdermilk, op. cit., Appendix, p. v.

Soldier by leaving his Company, or by words or Gestures expressing Fear shall suffer death...."[8] "... James Anderson of Col. Dunbar's Regiment who was tryed by ye General Court Martial is ordered 1,000 lashes with a Cat and Nine Tails...."[9] For drunkenness, a soldier received two hundred lashes without benefit of a court martial.[10]

Many of the frustrations and tensions were aggravated by the almost complete absence of recreation and women. One looks in vain for reports about recreational activity. Once in a while, there are small statements about holiday celebrations in which food, drinking, and singing are mentioned. Also cards were played—sometimes involving gambling. But gambling was discouraged by many officers.

Each company was permitted to have between four and eight women to help with the cooking, laundry and to serve in the hospital. In the absence of feminine gentleness, brutality became the norm. But there were times when women were part of the problem. On one occasion, Washington was forced to reprimand Captain John Ashby and his wife for "irregularities" at Ashby's Fort. In a very direct letter, Washington threatened immediate punishment unless the situation was corrected. He wrote,

> I am very much surprized to hear of the great irregularities which were allowed of in your Camp. The Rum, although sold by Joseph Coombs, I am credibly informed, is your property. There are continual Complaints to me of the misbehavior of your Wife; who I am told sows sedition among the men; and is chief of every mutiny. If she is not immediately sent from the Camp, or I hear any more Complaints of such irregular Behavior upon my arrival there; I shall take care to drive her out myself, and suspend you.[11]

[8]Ibid., p. VIII.
[9]Ibid., p. XII.
[10]Ibid., p. XLI.
[11]W. W. Abbot (ed.), op. cit., vol. II, p. 241.

A candid assessment of life at Fort Loudoun should be free of romanticism. Life was harsh and grim, an endurance contest which left cruel marks on many there. In some respects, it was an improvement over the more isolated forts because it was part of a village which in 1753 boasted of "about 60 houses, which are poorly built."[12] The town must have grown some by the time the fort was under construction because there were a number of ordinaries (taverns) in operation. They posed a problem for Washington in maintaining decorum.

> As every method hitherto practised has been found ineffectual to restrain the paltry tippling houses and Ginn-shops in this town, from selling liquor, contrary to orders, to the Soldiers, to the Detriment of His Majesty's Service, and irreparable loss of their own Health—It is hereby expressly ordered, that as many men as the Tents will contain, do immediately encamp; and all the rest, except those in the Hospital, be on Monday, new quartered upon Brinker, Heath and Lemon; who are charged not to sell more than a reasonable quantity of liquor, and at reasonable rates to each man per day—as they will answer the contrary. And any Soldier or Draught who is found drinking in any of the other houses, or is known to purchase, by direct or indirect means, any liquor from the other places; or shall be found ever going into, or sitting down in any of the other houses, without giving a sufficient excuse why he did so—shall immediately receive 50 lashes without benefit of a Court Martial....[13]

Living at Fort Loudoun was very directly influenced by the pressure exerted by the French and their Indian allies. We need now to take a look at the tragic story of a native population being squeezed tightly between the armed forces of the two European empires bent on conquest. It is a story of using and being used to advance the interest of empire on one side and of self-preservation on the other. It is also a story of much humanly inflicted suffering and death—another blight on the history of mankind.

---

[12]Garland R. Quarles, op. cit., p. 4.
[13]W. W. Abbot (ed.), op. cit., vol. III, pp. 338-99.

V

The Indian: Friend and Foe

It has often been suggested that this fourth in a series of wars between France and England has inappropriately been named, "The French and Indian War." The more neutral term, "Seven Years' War," as it was known in Europe, might be more accurate in view of the fact that each major power had alliances with those Indian tribes

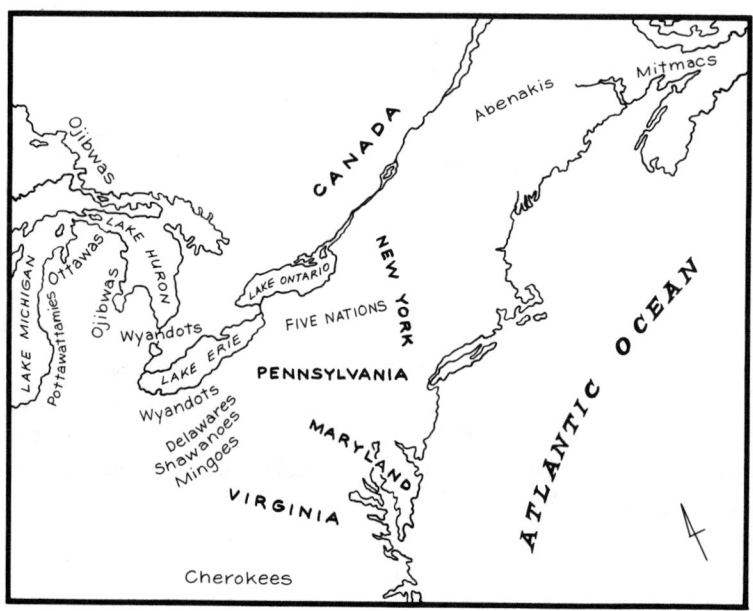

Location of several Indian tribes during the French and Indian War.

[1]Francis Parkman, op. cit., adapted from inside cover.

which they could bribe, cajole or threaten to "take up the hatchet" against their enemies.

The foregoing map shows the location of various Indian tribes during the period of study. It can be seen that those tribes inhabiting the Ohio region are most likely to be a problem to Virginians. Most of them were Algonquin and were friendly to the French.

Aligned with the British (except when neutral), were the Iroquois, composed mostly of the Five Nations (later Six Nations when joined by the Tuscaroras) along with the Cherokees and Catawbas. It should be remembered that tribes migrated either by choice or by external pressure so that maps spell out only general and temporary locations of tribes.

There is evidence that Shawnees lived in the vicinity of Winchester before the outbreak of the French and Indian War.[2] But they had vacated the Shenandoah Valley, making it a "no man's land."[3] This parallels reports of Indian activity in nearby Maryland. A long-time student of Maryland Indians asserts that,

> In their efforts to accommodate to the continued presence of these intruders and preserve some semblance of their traditional culture, the Indians sought legal counsel, waged war and finally resigned themselves to reservations. All to no avail. By 1756 it was estimated that only 140 Indians remained in Maryland. Many of the smaller, lesser known tribes had been forced to disperse and were later absorbed into other tribes; others simply vanished, leaving no evidence about their fate.[4]

The relentless pressure of land-hungry Europeans had taken a deadly toll.

After Braddock's defeat, and under prodding by the French, Indians began to infest the frontiers of Virginia making no exception for Winchester. Washington endeavored to make allies of those Indians who saw an ad-

---

[2]William M. Gardner, *Lost Arrowheads and Broken Pottery*, p. 93.
[3]Ibid., p. 90.
[4]Frank W. Porter III, *Indians in Maryland and Delaware*, p. IX.

vantage to giving their support to the British. He was partially successful in recruiting Cherokees, Catawbas and Nottoways to his cause.

In view of the threat that French expansion raised against Virginia's interests, Governor Dinwiddie planned a conference.

> ... for an early fall 1753 meeting to be held in Winchester between the chiefs and sachems of the Six Nations, and a Commission headed by Col. William Fairfax. ... Although they were expected in Winchester on August 20th, it was not until the 10th of September that their interpreter, Andrew Montour, arrived, reporting that the redskins delegation was then four miles away....
>
> At about 6:00 P.M. the Indians—ninety-eight men, women and children—came into sight.[5]

A week long series of meetings failed to produce the desired results. Exchanges of belts of wampum and other gifts by the Indians for guns, ammunition and other supplies by the whites at least resulted in a spirit of accord.[6] Later, Washington had similar conferences with the Indians to win their support as guides and warriors. One of these involved the Tuscarora Indians on August 1, 1756, at Winchester. Washington gave this message:

> To King Blunt, Capt. Jack, and the rest of the Tuscarora Chiefs—Brothers & Friends.
>
> This will be Delivered you by our Brother Tom, a Warrior of the Nottoways, who with others of that Nation, have distinguished themselves in our service this summer, against our cruel and perfidious Enemys. The intent of this, is, to assure you of our real Friendship and Love—and to confirm and Strengthen that chain of Friendship, which has subsisted between us for so many ages past, a Chain like ours, founded on Sincere Love, and Friendship, must be strong and lasting, and will I hope endure while Sun & Stars give light.[7]

Washington then embellishes his appeal with a reminder of French atrocities.

---

[5]Stuart E. Brown, Jr., *The Story of Thomas 6th Lord Fairfax*, pp. 125-6.
[6]Ibid., p. 127.
[7]W. W. Abbot (ed.), op. cit., vol. III, p. 308.

> Brothers, you can be no Strangers to the many Murders & Cruelties, Committed on our Country Men & Friends, by that False and Faithless people the French, who are constantly endeavoring to corrupt the minds of our Friendly Indians—and have Stirrd up the Shawnee & Delawares, with severall other nations to take up the hatchet against us....[8]

He then closed his address with a promise of arms, ammunition and other necessaries for making war. This was sealed with a string of wampum.[9]

Washington displayed his knowledge of the proper way to conduct business with his allies. The exchange of wampum was an integral part of Indian ceremony. "There were two kinds of wampum: white and black, both usually made from the hard-shelled clam or the whelk. Black wampum was made from the thick, purple part of the shell; being more difficult to make, it was twice as valuable as white wampum."[10] The same author asserts that "Wampum was sacred. For a speaker in council to hold a wampum belt in his hand was like a white man's laying his hand on the Bible and taking an oath."[11]

White wampum was a symbol of peace; black wampum, of grief or death. There were many variations of patterns in black and white, and size of the belt signified importance. To this must be added all of the ramifications of the way the belt was handled. Freeman points out that if a warrior threw the belt on the ground in a certain way he was professing sincerity, but when thrown another way, it was a declaration of war.[12] The number of strings or belts exchanged at a conference also symbolized importance. Henry Bouquet's papers disclose instances of six strings exchanged[13] or even nine on one occasion.[14]

[8]Ibid., p. 308.
[9]Ibid., p. 309.
[10]Paul A. W. Wallace, *Indians in Pennsylvania*, p. 56.
[11]Ibid., p. 56.
[12]Douglas Southall Freeman, *George Washington*, vol. I, pp. 296-97.
[13]Donald H. Kent, et. al., *The Papers of Henry Bouquet*, vol. III, p. 27.
[14]Ibid., pp. 507-11.

A Wampum Belt.[15]

The presentation of wampum belts was accompanied by oratorical flourishes which make modern day speeches look tame by comparison. At the Easton Conference in 1758, agreements were sealed by the governor of Pennsylvania who took a large white belt of wampum and declared, "By this belt we renew all our treaties; we brighten the chain of friendship; we put fresh earth to the roots of the tree of peace, that it may bear up against every storm, and live and flourish while the sun shines and the rivers run."[16] To this was added another dramatic surge, "By this belt we heal your wounds; we remove your grief; we take the hatchet out of your heads; we make a hole in the earth, and bury it so deep that nobody can dig it up again."[17]

Washington not only wanted to have the support of Indians; he wanted to incorporate some of their style and tactics of warfare. Having failed to influence Braddock in this regard, he was more successful on his second attempt to take Fort Duquesne. But this did not mean that he was not aware of the temperamental character of Indians. Because they knew how important they were to British success, they sometimes made demands for presents that Washington thought to be unreasonable. He once wrote, "They are the most insolent, most avaricious and most dissatisfied wretches I have ever had to deal with."[18] On another occasion he offered this opinion, "I

[15]Paul A. W. Wallace, op. cit., p. 56.
[16]Francis Parkman, op. cit., p. 391.
[17]Ibid., p. 391.
[18]Douglas Southall Freeman, op. cit., vol. II, p. 247.

cannot conceive the best white men to be equal to them in the woods; but I fear they are too sensible of their high importance to us to render us any very acceptable service."[19] Washington, as well as many other British and colonial leaders, became well aware of the unpredictable and vengeful behavior of their native allies.

A word is now due about the atrocities committed by Indians against their white invaders during this war. The instances are manifold and the documentation on Indian brutalities are easily obtained. They are shocking to normal sensitivities. But it must be pointed out, that whites were equally capable of atrocities.

Indian leaders were perceptive enough to see that regardless of who won the war, they would be under the domination of Europeans. In point of fact, the British, in the long run, were more of a threat to the Indian than the French. The French fur trade did not require settlement, nor with it a tendency to continually expand into Indian hunting ground. The British settlers, on the other hand, had an insatiable appetite for land.

The point was clearly made by the Onondaga Chief, Red Head, at an Iroquois council in 1755. He spoke,

> We are being destroyed by little pieces. Everywhere there are bites taken from us and they are like the bites of the mosquito—not felt until after the bite has been taken and there is no enemy there to slap, only a hole where once there was a part of us.
>
> We wanted no white men in our lands, but then we sold the edges of our land to them, English and French both, and they were not content, but began to eat into us more. We let them build fur-trading posts where we could sell what we work together and thus be able to buy the goods we need, but somehow these posts grow like living things and before we have turned around they are become forts and we are shut out of them and the land around them is suddenly no longer ours. . . . It is their war, yet it is our chiefs and our warriors who die and our lands which are lost. This must stop. . . . No more can we support white men, French or English, for they both have a design to kill us all.[20]

[19]Ibid., p. 322.
[20]Allan W. Eckert, *Wilderness Empire*, pp. 398-99.

It is not very edifying to dwell upon the many variations of gruesome cruelty which abound from frontier accounts. But the record would be incomplete without some notice of these barbarities. Each frontier fort has stories of a nearby family being slaughtered (along with livestock, poultry and pets) and a heart-rending account of a baby having its brains bashed out against a tree.

Those who were not killed were forced to march long distances to their captors' camps where they were brutalized until they died in agony. Torture included having their eyes gouged out, strips of skin cut from their body, joints removed and being burned alive.

Some were forced to run the gauntlet. This involved running through a double line of Indians to a specified point while their tormentors hit them with sticks, clubs or any object available. If they survived this ordeal, they were adopted by the tribe and then treated with great kindness. Sometimes, a squaw could take the victim as a replacement for their lost warrior husband. It is reported that captured children were frequently adopted and treated as though a member of the tribe.

If one recoils from some of the more lurid stories, there is one which, by far, overshadows these—the stories of cannibalism. Following is an interesting account of the great warrior, Pontiac, being upbraided by another chieftain because the Ottawa chief encouraged this grizzly custom among his braves.

> But as for you, Pontiac, you have taken prisoners upon the lake and upon the river, and after having brought them to your camp you have killed them and drunk their blood and eaten their flesh. You did it not in the manner of our—and your—custom, immediately after battle, when the flesh of the enemy is devoured so that you make take onto ourselves his strength and courage. No! You did it deliberately, when the time for custom was past. Is the flesh of men good for food? No! One eats only the flesh of deer and other animals which the Master of Life has placed on the earth for that purpose.[21]

[21] Allan W. Eckert, *The Conquerors*, p. 454.

Here we see at once the rationale for cannibalism and what is regarded as an abuse of the custom.

There is an attribute of the Indian which has attracted much attention—the capacity for cunning and deceit. Perhaps the unequal contest into which they were cast incubated and nurtured an expected human capability to a high level as an aid to survival. These qualities proved valuable when it is realized that ten of the thirteen British outposts were overtaken by the Indians in Pontiac's war.

A successful use of cunning occurred on June 2, 1763, at Fort Michilimackinac. A friendly game of lacrosse was in progress between the Chippewas and Sacs. Suddenly, one of the warriors scooped up the ball in the racket and heaved it toward the front gate of the fort. Both teams ran to that spot to be the recipients of knives, tomahawks, clubs and guns hidden under the blankets of squaws who had taken a strategic position at the gate. The surprise made an easy slaughter of those within—and a plentiful supply of scalps.[22]

The above event also reveals a reaction to what Pontiac saw to be the real problem faced by the Indian—dependency. His effort to shake off this dependency of European products came too late. The European was too entrenched and too strong, while the Indian was too dependent to make a successful break—especially with regard to guns and gunpowder.

One has but to look at the inventory of European goods for sale or exchange at a fur or trading post to see the extent of Indian dependency upon the white man. The following partial list is from Fort Bedford.[23]

  20 guns with locks
  21 Dozen & 8 Scalping Knives
   8 Pound of Vermilion
  4-1/2 Pound of Black & White Beads
  46 Pipe Tomahawks
  6000 White Wampum
  99 Dozen & 8 Glasp Knives

[22]Ibid., pp. 349 ff.
[23]Donald H. Kent, et al, *The Papers of Henry Bouquet,* Vol. III, pp. 4-5.

Since the stakes were high, a continent and its resources, it should not be surprising that brutality, cruelty and suffering would reach high levels. Both contestants in this war and their Indian allies on both sides regularly incited and participated in these barbarities. Scalping illustrated this point.

Scalping was taken for granted by almost all concerned. One exception was the Quakers who wanted the Indians to be treated kindly, and who would not support the war effort. But, in their refusal to provide for the protection of frontier families, they left these areas wide open to Indian attacks. Their pacifism undoubtedly contributed to the death of many frontier settlers. Most states paid a bounty for scalps.

In a letter to George Washington, Governor Robert Dinwiddie wrote:

> I hear 400 Cherokees are come to our assistance, but I have no Express from Co. Lewis. I have provided Arms sufficient for them; I ordered them directly to Winchester, & if they are with you, I think You shou'd send them out in Parties a Scalping, & let them know they will receive 10$ for every Scalp or Prisoner they make take....[24]

There was an interesting incident at Fort Cumberland in which Indian cunning failed to achieve its goal. A Shawnee warrior, Kill-buck, well known as a source of trouble, was possessed with a more-than-usual thirst for revenge toward the inhabitants of the namesake of the Duke of Cumberland. Several strategem had failed to work and so, deceit was the last resort. Kill-buck approached the fort gates with his warriors close at hand, all making gestures of friendship and requesting admission. Entrance was permitted but with a surprise. Just inside the gate, Kill-buck and his warriors faced a line of loaded guns and a pair of quickly closed gates. The ruse had failed. There, "Kill-buck and his chiefs were seized and disarmed, and were then dressed in petticoats; the

---

[24] W. W. Abbot (ed.) op. cit., vol. III, p. 405.

gates were opened, and they were driven forth with jeers and laughter by the soldiers, who taunted them with being squaws and old women."[25]

When we look at the other side of the coin, we are again confronted with an ugly picture. Brutality, it seems, was equally dispersed. After Braddock's defeat, the new French commander of Fort Duquesne, Captain Dumas, claimed to have,

> ... succeeded in ruining the three adjacent provinces, Pennsylvania, Maryland, and Virginia, driving off the inhabitants, and totally destroying the settlements over a tract of country thirty leagues wide, reckoning from the line of Fort Cumberland.... The enemy has lost far more since the battle than on the day of his defeat.[26]

This boast was probably not far from the mark and must have inflicted untold suffering on the frontier settlements of the three colonies named.

But there is another story which must rank high in the catalogue of sins which took place in 1763 at Fort Pitt (formerly Fort Duquesne). It will come as a shock to those who think germ warfare a recent contrivance. The followers of Pontiac had placed the fort under seige for some time. To get relief, it was suggested that it might be possible to infect the savages with smallpox germs. There is some debate about who actually conceived the idea of spreading the epidemic, but the infected blankets from the fort hospital were sent with the approval of General Amherst and Colonel Henry Bouquet.[27] The primary target was the Delawares. The plan was successful and an epidemic followed resulting in the death of some Delaware chiefs as well.[28]

It is not amiss at this point to raise the question as to whether the savagery of the tomahawk is on a lower level of morality than the barbarism of germ warfare. In any case,

[25] Will H. Lowdermilk, op. cit., p. 212.
[26] Francis Parkman, op. cit., pp. 192-93.
[27] Francis Jennings, op. cit., p. 438.
[28] Ibid., p. 447.

it is only fair to set the cases of cruelty alongside the many contributions the Indian has made to our culture. These make an imposing list, and must be given proper recognition.

Epilogue

A Note About Washington and "The Winchester Connection"

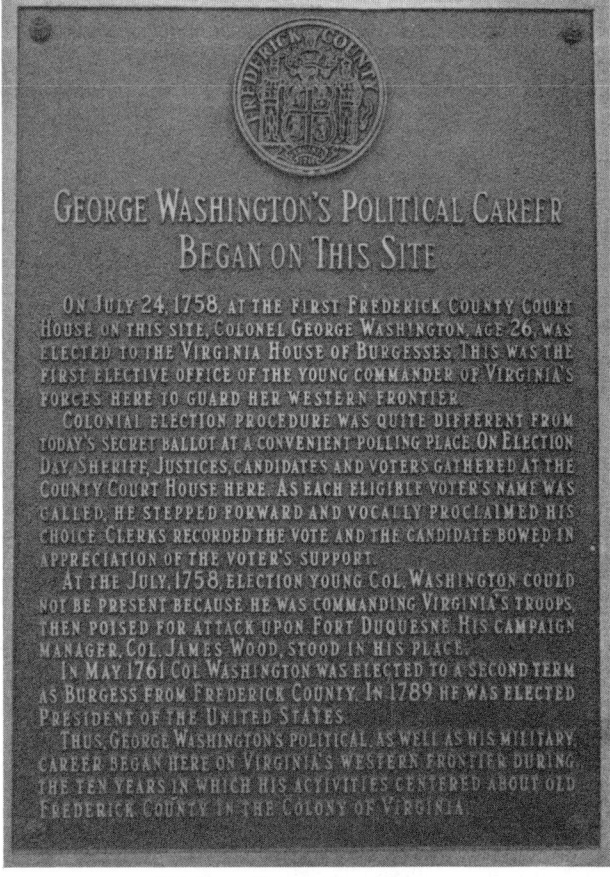

Citation—Front of courthouse
Winchester, Virginia.

From the preceding statement, it is obvious that Winchester is proud to be so intimately associated with the early career of George Washington. He came to Winchester at the age of sixteen as an energetic and enterprising student of the art of surveying with a budding thirst for land. After a ten-year association, he left a seasoned veteran of military campaigns and all the marks of maturity.

Washington reported in his diary of his first visit to Frederick Town (later to be called Winchester) on March 16, 1748.

> We set out early and finish'd about one oclock and then traveell'd up to Frederick Town where our baggage came to us we cleaned ourselves (to get rid of Y. Game we had catched the Night before) and took a Review of Y. town and thence returned to our Lodgings where we had a good Dinner prepared for us Wine and Rum Punch in Plenty and a good feathed bed with clean sheets which was a very agreeable regale.[1]

The surveying party, which included the young George William Fairfax, surveyed in the area until the middle of April before returning home.

In just a little more than a year (July 31, 1749), young Washington was authorized to practice surveying. With characteristic energy, he applied the skills of his new trade in Northern Virginia. But he did complain to a friend about the inconveniences of frontier living and assured "Richard" that "... a good Reward and Dubbleloon[2] is my constant gain every Day that the Weather will permit my going out and sometime Six Pistoles[3] ... "[4]

When possible, young Washington slept in Frederick Town. Local tradition has it that Washington used a small building on the corner of Braddock and Cork streets, now referred to as Washington's Office or Washington's Headquarters. It is said that Washington used the middle portion of the structure that now is supposed to have three distinct sections. This is doubted by some, however.

[1]Garland R. Quarles, op. cit., pp. 3-4.
[2]Dubbleloon or Dubloon—Spanish coin worth about $14.00.
[3]Pistole—Spanish coin worth about $3.50.
[4]W. W. Abbot (ed.), op. cit., vol. I, pp. 3-4.

Sketch of Washington's office.

In any event, Washington's industry paid off, and his earnings were quickly invested in good land which he selected during his travels. By early 1753, near his twenty-first birthday, Washington had acquired over four thousand acres.[5] About the same time, Washington became a major when he took the oath as adjutant for the southern district of Virginia.[6] This was undoubtedly a remarkable set of achievements for so young a man; but, on reflection, only a sign of better things to come.

For the next five years, Washington was in and out of Winchester, going to and from campaigns, trips to Williamsburg and Mt. Vernon, or missions of one kind or another. It will be recalled that he made stops at Winchester in 1753, on the way to Le Bouef; again, he stopped in 1754, on the way to "The Forks" and then in 1755, when traveling with the ill-fated Braddock.

[5]Freeman, op. cit., vol. I, p. 269.
[6]Ibid., p. 268.

With the frontiers of Virginia facing onslaughts from the incoming Indians, Washington was again pressed into service as "Colonel of the Virginia Regiment and Command-in-Chief of all the Forces now raised and to be raised for the Defense of His Majesty's Colony...."[7] Winchester was to be the place for the new commander's headquarters because it was "the highest place of rendezvous which is exposed to the enemy...."[8] He arrived there on September 14, 1755.

Between this date and until Washington left with the campaign to retake Fort Duquesne in 1758, he was busy building Fort Loudoun and engaged in the many details of building an adequate defense system for Virginia.

This ambitious young officer was also interested in politics. In 1755, he entered the contest for Burgess from Frederick County and was defeated. In 1758, while committed to the Forbes expedition, Washington again announced his interest to be a candidate. This time fortune was on his side, and he now added to his accomplishments the title of Burgess of Frederick County. Washington's campaign manager, Lieutenant Charles Smith, reported that he supplied 28 gallons of rum punch, 34 gallons of wine, 46 gallons of beer and 2 gallons of cider royal to the voters on election day. This cost the new delegate thirty-nine pounds and six shillings.[9]

After the Duquesne expedition, Washington made his way, via Winchester, to Mt. Vernon. Sick and exhausted, he made his way to a home that seemed to elude him. He was now twenty-seven years of age.

Douglas Southall Freeman gives a penetrating analysis of Washington at this point in his life.[10] He is quite frank in suggesting weaknesses, but also fair in pointing out the strengths. One clue as to how far Washington had matured in his capacity as a leader is indicated by a

---

[7]Garland R. Quarles, op. cit., p. 18.
[8]Ibid., p. 18.
[9]Ibid., p. 41.
[10]Op. cit., vol. II, pp. 368-99.

letter from his subordinate officers in December of 1758, when he left camp for Mt. Vernon. In part it read, "... as you have hitherto been the actuating soul of the whole corps, we shall at all times pay the most invariable regard to your will and pleasure...."[11] This is indeed a worthy tribute to the great Virginian.

[11]Ibid., p. 399.

Appendix I

American Advices.

PHILADELPHIA, *May* 27. In a Letter from Dumfries in Virginia, dated the 13th Inſtant, there is Advice, that at Winchester, and about it, the Inhabitants ſeemed to be in a good Degree reſtored to their uſual Tranquility, moſt of the People who had left their Plantations having returned to them. That near 1000 of the Militia were aſſembled from the adjacent Counties, but it was thought they would ſoon be diſcharged, the Cauſe of their being called together ſeeming to be removed. And that Col. Waſhington was to ſet out for Fort Cumberland on the 10th of this Month, whoſe Corps were to be made up 1500 by the 20th, by a Draught of the Militia throughout the Colony, who were all able-bodied young Men, and to be draughted by Ballot, every twentieth to go, or ſend a Man in his Room.

From *Bath* (England) *Journal,* July 26, 1756.

This is a contemporary description of the state of affairs in the vicinity of Winchester, Virginia, some time after Braddock's defeat. It reflects the unsettled conditions created by threats of French and Indian ravages while Washington was trying to build a system of defense for the colony. The account is now on display at Washington's office at Winchester, Virginia.

Appendix II

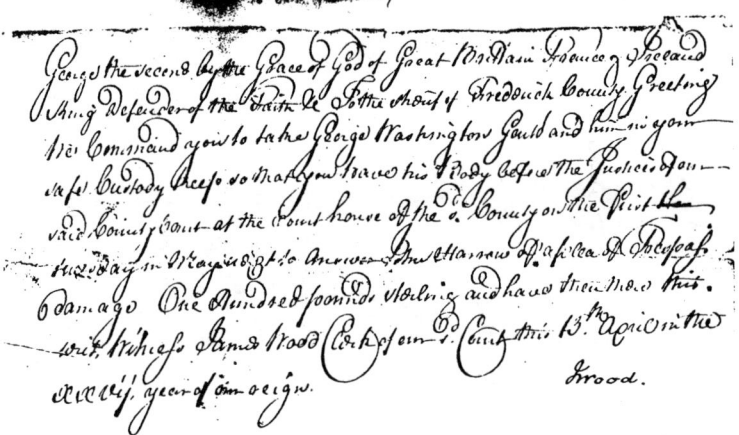

A warrant for the arrest of George Washington.

This is one of three warrants in the author's possession. It seems that citizens did not take kindly to having their horses and wagons pressed into service—even if it was for their own protection.

Appendix III

Three notices from the sheriff that Washington could not be found.

60

Appendix IV

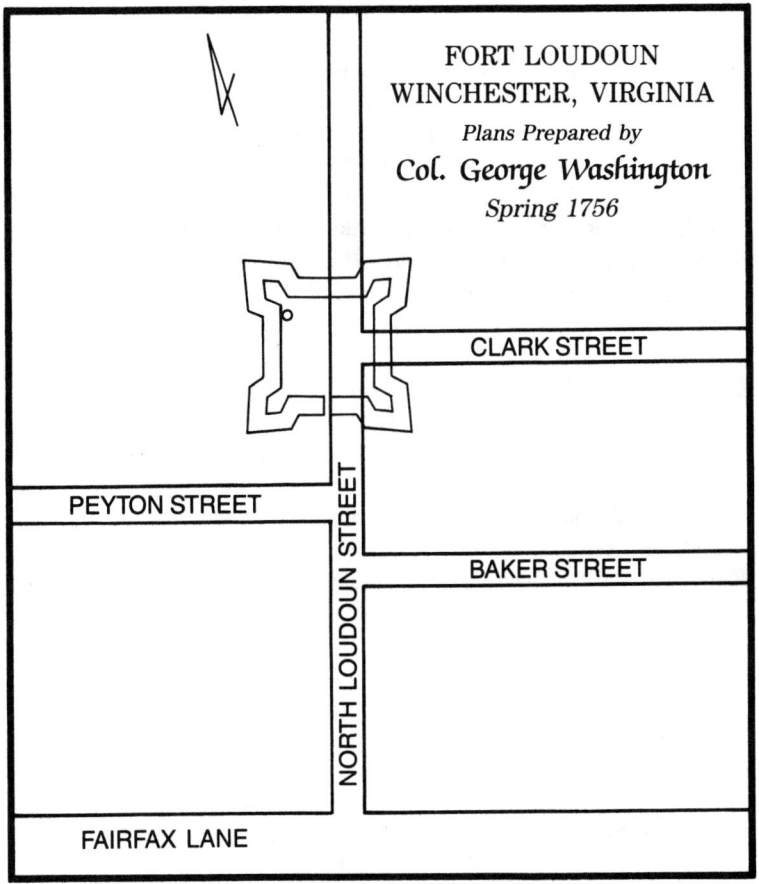

SITE OF FORT LOUDOUN
Winchester, Virginia
Prepared by Lois M. Newman
City Engineer's Office, Winchester, Virginia
April, 1989

Bibliography

BOOKS

Abbot, W. W. (ed.), *The Papers of George Washington*, Vols. 1-5, Charlottesville: University Press of Virginia, 1983.

Ansel, William H. Jr., *Frontier Forts Along the Potomac and Its Tributaries*. Parsons, W.Va.: McClain Printing Co., 1974.

Brown, Stuart E. Jr., *Virginia Baron: The Story of Thomas 6th Lord Fairfax*. Berryville, Va.: Chesapeake Book Co., 1965.

Cartmell, T. K., *Shenandoah Valley Pioneers and Their Descendants*. Berryville, Va.: Chesapeake Book Co., 1963.

Eckert, Allan W., *The Conquerors*. New York, N.Y.: Bantam Books, 1970.

Freeman, Douglas Southall, *George Washington*. Vols. 1-2, New York, N.Y.: Charles Scribner Sons, 1948.

Frye, Dennis F. (et al. eds.), *The James E. Taylor Sketchbook*. Dayton, Ohio: Morningside House, 1988.

Gardner, William M., *Lost Arrowheads and Broken Pottery*. Manassas, Va.: Tru Tone Press, 1986.

Harrington, J. C., New Light on Washington's Fort Necessity. Richmond, Va.: The Eastern National Park and Monument Association, 1957.

Jennings, Francis, *Empire of Fortune*. New York, N.Y.: W. W. Norton and Co., 1988.

Kent, Donald H., *The French Invasion of Western Pennsylvania*. Commonwealth of Pennsylvania, Pennsylvania Historical and Museum Commission, 1981.

Kercheval, Samuel, *A History of the Valley of Virginia*, (6th ed.). Harrisonburg, Va.: C. J. Carrier Co., 1981.

Lowdermilk, Will H., *History of Cumberland, Maryland*. Baltimore, Md.: Regional Publishing Co., 1971.

McCardell, Lee, *Ill-Starred General*. Pittsburgh, Pa.: University of Pittsburgh Press, 1958.

O'Meara, Walter, *Guns at the Forks*. Pittsburgh, Pa.: University of Pittsburgh Press, 1979.

Parkman, Francis, *Montcalm and Wolfe.* New York, N.Y.: Atheneum, 1984.

Porter, Frank III, *Indians in Maryland and Delaware.* Bloomington, Ind.: Indiana University Press, 1979.

Stevens, S. K. (et al. eds.), *The Papers of Henry Bouquet.* Vols. 1-4, 1951-1978.

Wallace, Paul A. W., *Indians in Pennsylvania.* Harrisburg, Pa.: Pennsylvania Historical and Museum Commission, 1989.

Williams, Thomas J. C., *A History of Washington County, Maryland.* Vol. I, Hagerstown, Md.: John M. Runk and Q. R). Titsworth, 1906.

JOURNALS

Hough, Walter S., "Braddock's Road Through the Virginia Colony." Winchester-Frederick County Historical Society, Vol. 7, 1970.

Quarles, Garland R. "George Washington and Winchester, Virginia: 1748-1758." Winchester-Frederick County Historical Society, Vol. 8, 1974.

Miles, Lion G., "The Winchester Hessian Barracks." Winchester-Frederick County Historical Society, Vol. 3, 1988.

Word Index

Admiral Keppel, 17
Alexandria, 12
Ashby, John, 40
Beaujeu, Daniel, 19
Blainville, Celeron de, 3
bloody flux, 18, 37
Bouquet, Henry, 25, 37, 51
Braddock, Edward, 11, 12, 13, 14, 15, 16, 17, 19, 20, 21, 23, 25
cannibalism, 48
Catawbas, 18, 43, 44
Cherokees, 18, 43, 44
Conococheague, 15
Conogogee, 15
Contrecoeur, Captain, 19
Dagworthy, John, 27, 28
Delawares, 21, 51
Dinwiddie, Robert, 3, 4, 6, 7, 8, 16, 18, 26, 28, 39, 44, 50
Dumas, Captain, 19, 51
Dunbar, Thomas, 13, 15, 18, 22, 24
Dunbar's Camp, 18, 21
Forbes, John, 38
Fort Cumberland, 15, 17, 22, 24, 27, 30, 33, 50
Fort Duquesne, 9, 18, 19
Fort Loudoun, 31, 34, 35, 36, 41, 45, 67
Fort Necessity, 3, 10, 21
Fort Pitt, 51
Franklin, Benjamin, 14
French and Indian War, 1, 43
Half King, 9
Halkett, Peter, Sir, 12, 13
Hanbury, John, 4
Innes, James, 27
Iroquois, 5, 43
Joliet, 3

Jumonville, Coulon de, 9
Kill-buck, 50
La Salle, 3
Le Boeuf, 3, 7, 8
Legardeur, de St. Piere, 8
Loudoun, Lord, 29, 37
Marquette, 3
Michilimachinac, 49
Ohio Company, 4, 5
Orme, Robert, 16
Ottawas, 21
Pontiac, 49
Pontiac's Conspiracy, 35
Red Head, 47
scalping, 50
Scarouady, 23
Seven Years' War, 1, 43
Sharpe, Horatio, 27, 28
Shawnees, 21, 45
Shirley, William, 28
Six Nations, 43
spruce beer, 37
Stephen, Adam, 27, 30
Swearingen's Ferry, 17
The Forks, 3, 6
Turtle Creek, 19
Venango, 3, 6
Wampum, 44, 45, 46
Washington, George, 6, 7, 8, 9, 10, 12, 15, 16, 17, 18, 22, 25, 26, 27, 28, 29, 30, 31, 33, 37, 38, 39, 40, 44, 45, 46, 54, 55
Washington's Office, 55, 58
Williams, Thomas, J. C., 15
Williamsburg, 6, 8, 29
Wills Creek, 6, 9, 11
Winchester, 26, 27, 28, 31, 33, 34, 38, 43, 44, 53, 54, 55, 56